Beneath: The Dark Sun

Beneath: The Dark Sun

By Nicholas A. Messenger

Poetry collection 2018-2021
Cover Art by Nicholas Messenger
"Mirror Chasm Libertine"
        -paper collage

Back cover
-Photo Cred
Kindness Photo Co

ISBN: 978-0-578-33673-2
Published by Nicholas Messenger

Dedicated to my son,
Emett David Messenger

Table of Contents

A Cold Visage

Back to age 12, my grandfather's funeral
where tears lined the pews, and moans on rafters
perch. I leaned over inspecting the powdered face;
he and I were no longer, but the shape remained
for them. That year became a circus of desperation
where I felt nothing. Where I wanted nothing,
nothing like the barrow inside. I knew silence
when the yelling abated. I would wait
for sleep became a casual affair, my mother couched
in their marriage's final days. She, seemingly quiet,
coveting freedom while He labored over so long
for love; however, he smelled his foolishness,
and it was lost pride he could not weld back together.
He cried once. I saw him
slamming the door to closet his wounds
Grecian marble pulled over my own
blank stare. It sound's muted
since she moved out. The house is no longer
a home. It is some place where the hurt resides
external to the cause. The walls decayed
with children cemented to the cold concrete
foundations because children are useful
in court. We were shuffled amongst the laundry,
our parents' grime in the lint trap, and still,
there are no fountains where a penny found is cast:
That place is beyond hope,
where wishes are half drowned.

The Group: Psychotic

I have been surrounded by liars, fakers, and deceivers, so long
I have forgotten what strangers are like. When around friends,
we tip-toe dangerously close to our mutual insecurities. Falling in love
with pseudo-anonymity, because each knows what questions not to ask;
that absolution through distraction is why our paths keep meeting
on the porch, just inside the gate telling others to beware. It is safe
to dilute our self, only just enough, so the veneer is not too opaque
as when phone calls are not answered and the stench of hops floats
like unwashed urinals in men's restrooms;
we put on a show, pissing on the floor
between the fences separating our falseness. We are our clothes,
twisting and turning to benefit our profile.
Each of us will say only what we wish to share,
but we all see that unique brokenness.
The field musicians are suturing the lips; without them
all I hear is slammed doors in angst and too long silences,
violence rearing just below the surface. The color of friendship,
it is a grey area.
I met two in an alleyway across the asphalt, behind grey-green trashcans
that had so much trash inside our pot smelled sweet. As good as fresh roadkill—
That skunk, the smoke billowing over the cinderblock walls,
staining our fingers like some adhesive. We found each other appealing,
and memories are still alive, like dying echoes brought back to life
whenever the two resuscitate those issues. They held papier-Mache
decorated with unique views on past events. Those are war medals
pinned over the places the world hurt us—
Everyone is a veteran to PTSD in our neighborhood. An epidemic,
achieving subliminally more damage than impoverishment ever could,
these scenarios play again. And again, those two relive that addiction,
which seems to have outlasted their fight with cocaine,

again, that neighborhood stain flashed in the light of their words;
it is metallic, the same color as the barrel of your father's gun,
tasting like money that has traded a thousand hands.

4 years later, I returned. For the most part they came back
and in many ways, we were drawn together again. It wasn't the drugs,
because we stopped using. It was as if we were taking hold of opportunity,
strangling her with fervor. A step back on the concrete
boots found solid ground. Stamping the stone, trapping a primal heat, there
we found that we cared. Death was as far as we could cast those dice
tumbling through the unknown,
but maturing with a slick, black mold; They carried that baggage tied to a rope.
It dragged behind, that weight ever growing;
getting closer every time they wound their slack around their necks, looking back,
the tension choked them each new tide in our beach-less city.

The Christian, cooked his way from Europa, bringing his sandals.
And while he wore the pleats upon his crown, he never felt their weight
like he felt the burns on his arms.
The same scars were hieroglyphs decorating his master's hands
as he earned his creed. However; The Christian was an affluent beggar,
a naivety which took advantage in singlemindedness. Perpetually blind
to the hurt he causes in his invasiveness. He was generous,
enough to return, banking on taking bets on the horse races;
he wagered his friendship for the temptress who belonged to another,
so their entanglement was enough to drive us apart.
Now, he plays another game…
…cooking again, like it was his first time in the kitchen, he caught a young bird.
Without care he fled the law,
dragging this whistling dove. She has the tongue of a curmudgeon,
like him when it comes to tipping at restaurants. A mutual narcissism—
it's passionless when you live under your parent's auspices,
suckling the maternal tit. The taste is similar.
As are apartments in Deutschland and the warmth of a girl's breath,

they linger in the back of his throat. The acidic burn of white-collar medicine,
it creates a pocket where The Christian keeps his secrets. Behind the vanity
with the same shape as her narrow lips when she asks where he's been,
his smiling is false as the image inside the mirror. Mounted there on a pedestal,
the two of us piled quality, but neither of us saw the other as an equal.

There is another specimen amongst the group, and it shines like a crystal,
allowing its knowledge to be read. Like it or not, that Ruby was desperate to show you,
assimilating affectation to subdue its rawest elements. Overflowing with facts
like that was everything. I've heard the same stories, but I don't acquiesce to dogma.
That stone's religion was the story it wove; it was more interested in being admired,
educating in exchange. Disagreement was not an option,
people don't verbalize with gems and the tiny, gift-wrapped packaging.
Ideas left on top of the ice box, behind the cereal and next to the liquor,
that fruit spoiled. Those words, caught in the throat, it is congratulating itself after all.
Your little comical inquiries could not be slipped in between it retorting.
One-way conversations are like that.
It tells all the same stories because it likes hearing them
as if someone else was retelling those victories,
leaving loneliness unsaid. That is why it drinks;
No one can bare to tell it, "No,"
because that would show too much weakness.
That group of sheep
bleating in unison. A chorus that never let it be vulnerable.
And…
there is synchronicity in my wake. I trade groups and homes,
and when I do, the vacuum is so loud its bellowing draws in ugly personalities,
swarming as ants do. The carcass consumed in days of China White;
That porcelain is sharp,
and pungent is their desire. Those two shared an addiction
that was called our dichotomy. Hiding when I call,
listening to messages days later. You would know
I was looking. That gaze searching through your facial expressions
between you licking your teeth, the action painting your smile

like salt on the wave's crest, bleached white, riding that tide unseen
by friends, until it's there in your shallows. Your upper lips, as chapped as dryer sheets
it moves over the gums the way oil fires sit right above the surface
waiting to inhale everything you own. Caviar candy preserves well,
but while people don't notice the holes in your nose, where you keep your money,
they see the empty wells in your soul. Right behind the glossy, parched eyes,
you two cut something besides the coke.

Racing: to Stir the Ocean Awake

We drove with the wind on our necks
like that red car held possibility. Along its treads,
where our footpath prevailed against the odds,
rocks spun out along the asphalt driveway. Disintegrating,
obstacles are shouldered to the wayside. Not slowing you down
in your sandals, laughing. All the while I was far from it,
in the background; I thought that I held the controls behind the shifting gears.

I never knew beauty like when I saw you,
digging stones from my sides. They hurt me
the way you asked me where I was. I have a dark guilt
where I hear you stumble in my shadow;
the lights are not on the wall. They were unexpected,
turning red, where before they had always been green
like your mother's eyes.

And hearing them shout—Her tongue burning hot
when we played at night. Not afraid to say it was home
in the distance. That Porch facing out towards everything,
we saw anything coming our way. Within the border of oleanders and mailboxes,
our trashcans on the front step, we watched that long hair fly
burnished gold in color to match his eyes. His whites remaking the moonlight
to the tide of his gait. He wove mystery enough to stir my world.

One time I took him to the park playground in summer. He was 5,
more willing to brave the heated oasis of youth, but it was abandoned
except for the homeless lingering in the passing shade of young trees.
This is a young town of old people. The parks told that history
as we walked its concrete ramparts. Flags billowed half-mast
observing a holiday only spoken of within library walls.

Still those tennis shoes broke fresh soil, underneath the grass,
never relying on the cleaver architecture to mark out his path.
And, in that moment—

He was resplendently blaspheming the Sun's strangled city,
its denizens alarmed at how his skin's static crackled
when he slid down the softened, plastic slide, alone.
Nothing is too big to conquer. He glows with optimism,
the light in the darkness,
consuming whatever loneliness couldn't sap.

I ran with him on occasion. My stride shook the ground,
making him slow down to turn. At the stump, speeding
we face off on the stretch to Uncle's house. The bearded,
beer drinking savant. He chided, just enough to toughen that skin.

He was soft as only only-children are,
while his flesh was touched by the Sun, forming a copper layer
barricade to intrusion. Even though his door was always open;
he was behind it. Waking early,
playing games while his parents slept. His vigor forming
in daylight, piercing the windowsill above his bed—
He showers the world with his silent yawns, loud enough to inspire gaps

taking in the morning air. He revels in the chill
under the neighboring Pecan forest. Their leaves fall
in piles, where the stray cats piss. We blow them,
like horns on ships passing, achieving space in the dark,
cold ground underneath the sparse light. Spreading our fingertips
deep into soft dirt. You are far too bold,
digging through the gravel I hide my darkness in.

Trying not to show the tears that come too easily,

you sort out more than is apparent, folding it into the leaves,

letting that depression die there between the veins,

as the sky softened to match their somber hue;

the rains brought hope. A kind only found in the desert,

when the colors of the wild grasses glow green with life,

climbing the trees to soak up the spray of the heavens—

Even the spines of saguaro reach out their claws

taking from us our fragility like savage beasts,

hording. Their wealth growing as slow as fingernails.

I never like saying, "Go," when he leaves my side. It is false,

because I savor the sound of the toy car's screech

around the bend, as he comes back. My position towards the Sun changing.

Before I could not find shade, but he is lavender after the storm,

fragrant and soothing to my lungs. He has become the breath I crave,

and forever wouldn't be long enough to share it.

Ideal Penetration

(Internal)

When Fucked by your ideas, I was not searching
behind the seed—my willingness in our union is
taking you within this blessed embrace? I am penetrated.
The vulnerability of my womb broken open
by our coupling, roots extending. Creating fissures in this vessel
Me, adorned with innocence. The gown I wore
the night before cannot shield my falseness.

I covet, the lace laboring to hold together—tenuous chastity,
it becomes taught. Struggling by progress under these auspices,
covenant is a sexual touch. Flashing, it blinds me. Me? I thought I was?
Ashamed by the swiftness, white sheets turn red, I fight
putting the dress back on, all the while I am guided.

With my persistence, words reach ears willing
to come to term with the way your touch moves
beyond sight—The garden in my belly is fertile.
In the light of darkness, these weddings are portraits
being torn like a cloud striking out violent over the sea,
without witness. It is always happening. Poison seeps,
with intent it makes skin oiled and softened in youth decay.

Tomorrow I will reach for a mirror to confirm my fear.
"I have become hideous with shame. His words.
His manhood has wrought a barrow of my virginity.
Where there is nothing beautiful, I will see. I must look."
The lifting of polished plastic is like being buried. Inch after inch
the angle catches my image, while the past chokes me with assumption.
Anticipation makes me shake, and the hurt solidifies
the grave. I place a headstone over those eyes, its shadow cast behind me

like the writing carved in effigy. It reads, 'Once fucked.
She died. Living again, married to the fucker.' Eyes always open,
hearing the voice of my husband. The mirror reflects
something unexpected, instead of being ugly.
I am something—New, and it is beauty.

That grave was really a chrysalis. Metamorphosis is taking place
under the archway of our vows, however intolerable, I am bathed in light
today. I find it good. When I became ready
the infant in my womb entered a family. Where it is preparing.
by shearing off the carapace made hard by fear; however it shines,
imperfect thought is burning upon the altar. This timely ritual is full of fucking.
After continually marrying the process, I always see. Its grace is accepting the terms.
It is part of my soul. It is my destiny to bare
something new. It is purification by rigors of internal struggle in becoming
as sublime as discovering a star. Where I forgot to look, was to you.

Trauma

I do not want the world to see, me, lost
in thought and perplexity. While outwardly exposed
I cannot adjust the camera into focus. I cannot relate
blurred lines around rape culture—While friends sit close,
in their monochrome nests, whispering
avarice enough to silence; Laughter enough to normalize it,
while the most studious predators do not look up the skirts. Secretly
they are trying to lull friends into accessing their confidence...
Their homes... Their children.
When it is ordinary, we have submerged our progeny
in graves at sea. This casual banality surrounding depths
vicious and shameful, it is like the coffins have bones for nails
burrowing inside the walls.
They let the light in as it floats before the inevitable,
fated to sink. Their color disappears into darkness. Somehow hiding trauma there,
an ocean's weight on our souls, holding us down in waves
bound by the wrist, like an umbilical cord. It is knotted up
because that is innocuous enough when the hurt is not discussed—
The oceans do not allow headstones because that is evidence
that every smile has the potential to be false.
Nothing can be believed, then
when teen suicides are covered as an overdose,
we all take a shot of Narcan to forget;
Restarting our pulmonary system because the heart does not
recognize the pain. It is written by trembling hands
in a sitcom. The actors are memorizing lines
to shadow nausea every time someone gets too close.
So, we don't need to relive those moments,
for there are so many, but no one sees
what can be left unsaid.

The Refuge Beyond the Needles Sting

Caustic junkies wear their nods. They are resting
with the left-over urine caked to their scalp;
flies eat their ambition, but insecticide was slammed
over their sleek, glassy eyes. They wait behind
closed lids and one-way mirrors. I watched those lepers,
their festering blood coursing, and I felt sad
when I saw those naked children running through it.
No shelter like the lime their parents buried them in.
I tried to change the channel. They were watching me,
while peeling the scabs from under fingernails, and I knew,
the Poppy floating down into the crib
found an artery. I tried to suck the poison,
my breath caught behind clenched teeth, but I was smiling.
My remorse displayed in those moments, seemingly
a macabre irony. I tasted the asphalt's tarry exterior, then;
My eyes betraying my addiction, I forgot to forget…

…the opium desires. It lingers in the air
like uneaten fruit, and its future is to spoil
the two-year-old. She slept like us, succumbing too.
Feverishly sleeping, life becomes bouts of light,
interspersed between the shaking hands. I fumble
another dose, oblivion rearing its black seduction
like waves heard but remaining unseen;
The camera lens doesn't catch the bruises
hidden under long sleeves,
keeping me complacent and afraid.

With A Glance

Longing eye's, drift across this place
towards a lonesome figure. Their eyes met,
thaumaturgy takes place. Souls dropped from Mercury's embrace;
Thrice great sandals carry the slough,
like shed metallic vessels, iniquities balance across
the rim of their anise laced cups.

Each vouchsafes their body, not their hearts
buried deep in intimate facades.
Transaction in vanity is tragic
drama, like the fold of skin stretched
along lines of her smile.
He could smell her through the smoke
built on Turkish fields. It drew him
down into her lust's ghostly perfume.

The door opened. Ushering in the rain's
cataclysm from outside their game.
The two shed coats. Mrs. replaced miss
forgetful of her vows. No shame, he had
a family. Battering against the window,
grey tears were drawn down silt, only
to be illumined by passing desires.

She smiled a different kind of smile,
like she had to hide. A five-year-old
childlike with the toy she covets,
playing with being innocent, until she looks
like her toy was not hers any longer.
It belongs to their moment—Sacrosanct.

He sees his misgivings
painted curbside. Outside the restaurant step
the streets gurgled mockeries. A vicious slander
are glances made under false pretenses?
They flow as marriage. Drawn from gutters,
that once shown golden on her finger.

She touched him with her eyes before this sewer
embraced the detritus, but the silver sheen seemed as pitch
when church bells toll hollow with laughter. A joke,
sardonic in niceties, like thunder. It reminded him
the flash was as brief as their fidelity.

Do sailors stare? Out of their port
across vast oceans and hurricanes between
their lovers and their home—do the masts fail
when winds beauty shreds the sail? They must
wonder if the hearth in the familial castle's burning;
Not to replace the darkness, but to cover her fear.

He might not return. He is guided by starlight.
It seeps under the door, into the bed
they made, portraits with only one side,
the other lies within an inch of the wall.
The only witness to the cracks this sin created.

Cycles of Attrition

Where the wound lay is internal. Living
while perfecting the disconnect, eternally hidden in laughter.
That distance burns every year, my arms looking like hatch-marks
counting the steps during the daily calendar dances.
Each dip a little deeper, like those downward spiral stones imitate
when submerged. They spin, each facet looking to reflect
the surface, bringing some of the sky's openness
to the deep. Eyes unwrap the warm, fleshy, pink coat
attracting sharks. The way blood does, rising to the surface,
drawing them in too close. The smell is human
under the red stripes, making it harder to swim
held under premises. Where breath is exhaustingly sought,
it's underground; It's underneath, and the only thing I let in.
These collars outstretched stories
selling my poison, the way radio hosts sell water beds;
soup kitchen gossip softening hearts to pity the wretch
sitting next to the tracks, looking for a home for the season.
Squatting because in a room full of addicts even sleep has speech
enough to beguile. Reason enough to stumble amongst the web, unseen,
where the psychotic sleep, afraid—
Sometimes conversation is forced, because sides are drawn;
fleshy borders around mental illness, barbed wire crucifixions
decorating the divide, with sickness on the other side,
where people isolate their fears. Creating space for culling
emotional response—serve them a dark lithium gaze
so sedation will police the ill. Castration by pill
for now. Our bodies parceled like tawdry items
raking in state checks, while the patient is homeless,
a veteran to the freeway onramps. Skin is textured and colored
like the Red Rocks, as craggy as wind worn sandstone.
The thousand faces of clemency behind cardboard signs and sharpies,
those hands are the high desert, brimming with desperation,

it runs over their fingertips, and beneath the surface

their veins are coursing arroyos. The network carries loss

like that man who passed, between a shopping center

entryway for commodities worth providing for. He was too old to care.

But no one will cry when his last breath happens, there

on his back fixing the gears of the bike above him

like a simpleton Michelangelo. Aluminum replacing plaster ceilings,

he toiled so close to G-d, stretched out on display.

He put down his tools 20 minutes before

someone noticed. His bike,

probably looked like it was for sale,

but J.D. had static, sightless eyes

staring wildly, searching for someone to ask, "Do you see me?"

Darkened Hearts
(Part 1)

The memory of you is rich in my mind. A dark reminiscence,
where the word love is more akin to loss. I lived through the fallout, barely
surviving that poison that you left behind in your wake. The outcome was unexpected,
because we never spoke in the real. Dabbling in mystery was a nightly affair,
apathy flooding me as I watched time lapse,
your voice reduced to silent clicks animated in my peripherals;
I didn't make conversation easy. It was nonexistent in the end,
like how my attempts at seduction ran dry. There was no reason
we remained together. Even though the color had drained
I know why I stayed, but I wish I knew why you did.

I remember that you didn't like me at first, but I took your hand
that night we first met. We danced, holding that static charge
between our fingers—the distance, felt before,
shattering as our attraction drew your breath on my face,
stirring something inside of us I never let go of.

The first time I saw snow was when visiting you. Getting off the bus,
there were snowflakes on that perpetual wind of Flagstaff,
drifting around my duffle-bag. You met me at the station. Your freckles deepening,
either because of the cold or the way the warmth of our lips radiated
down your spine. I wrote my passion there
when we kissed, feeling your heart tremble against my chest;
while in those arms, I never wanted to call another place home.

That night, sitting in the cemetery behind our future home together,
we shared a mutual fear. Among the masonic gravestones,
we fought the urge to bolt. The curl of your smile tempted me and the shadows behind,
but I quickly realized you had a soul unlocking my doors,
those fortifications built in adolescence.

It was time for me to feel the unreserved, your persistence guiding me
to that end. You drew a circle around us, instantly recognizable
as equal parts.

Like a nomad whose catchment camps have seasons,
I wandered along an icy skein of glass, my feet dragging,
until my home became wherever you led me. I never knew I was looking
for one. I didn't want to give up control, but you replaced my restraint
with a passion for your embrace. The same way that prisoners of war feel returning
over the borders almost lost to memory. I gave up that far away prison.

We were kids, only breaking into our friend's Parents' privacy,
on the weekend. Those homes would open their doors,
never a thought given to who would attend. That was neglect
when I went out to steal beer, leaving you alone.
My alcoholism consuming sense, I am sure I asked why
you two exited a bedroom upon my return,
but you never answered the questions I didn't ask.
You cried as we made love the next morning;
tensing up when the boy you loved shares the same wound,
your tears and hair were matted against my shoulder.
I got no answers—I did not understand that, until my own trauma;
silence is easier. Our scars far in the background,
they have names and faces and addresses—Why did we hurt each other
instead. I buried my guilt in a place I drank to forget,
because I never had the opportunity to trust
until you finally said it.
I never forgave myself for not knowing; For not protecting you
before you didn't love me anymore.

I left Phoenix in July, northbound. That windy cold called my name,

like serendipity had me on auto dial. Everything lined up,

with the shots on the railing poured slow. I watched the fireworks

outside the hotel, on the balcony, hearing the bursting

air pockets igniting. That sulfur was spread so thick upon the wind

I could not smell your hair beyond the burnt miasma.

But as I held your small frame in my arms,

That missing piece sticking out, you latched onto something,

not someone. I was a television that could be faced against the wall

every time you did not like your reflection. So, you bent the foil antennae

bringing only what you wished into focus. There were snowflakes on the screen,

like our apartment windows in Winter. The icy steps were underneath

a great stalactite hanging over from the rooftop runoff.

It fell every Spring, but did not crush me:

> like the casual way you finally brought up abortion

> like the lovers you enjoyed, hiding their smiles

> The pair were reasons for the other.

It's because of what I saw in the toilet, besides the obvious tissue.

It was not the vision of the child we were supposed to have. The child was pale

like me, floating in bloody water.

I lost that memory, of the hurt

you suffered, and I carried on oblivious.

Is it a question that can be brokered? Please ask her

boy or girl? Miscarriage or otherwise?

I did,

You were silent. Always…

silent like bus routes. The number of patrons rising exponentially each new stop,

but the lack of sound becomes deafening as bodies amass, muting their neighbors.

I was so close to where you hid your face. I was there, standing near the door

waiting for you to speak. You are telling me it was out stop, but I couldn't ring the bell.

Time elapsed, measured by the dissipating frost

fogging up my glasses every time you exhaled—there in isolation,

you carried so much weight, and I could not lift the baggage unseen.

And unknown to me, it grew

like bamboo digging into my side. The longer I stayed, the more segments formed

bricking up the circumference of your garden. You couldn't find your way out;

The exit sign had arrows directing traffic, but you stalled. Breaking the gears,

I had thought they would drive our lives, but the cogs in our mechanism didn't fit.

I would sit on the faded river-rock's second story, smoking

cigarette butts from the ashtray. The one I stole from the Mason Jar,

like the Lovecraftian collection I never returned to the library,

they were talismans I brought with me. Glowing with memory

like a mental note was left there between those timeless pieces;

Paper thick, that cord fluttered in my calloused hand. It is a feral Djinn

sifting through my life, and that spirit did not find much.

But then I had nothing to steal. I thought…

that night in the garage, when you were willingly honest,

breaking the one-sided lies

long after I found I was a vagabond,

drinking as if forgetfulness tasted best chilled.

I lingered in the forest. Thinking I could still see

the Sun glowing red behind the smoke.

The next season I found a better love

when the forest's hands could choke me no more.

You no longer tried and neither did I.

Ideal Penetration

(External)

When I fuck you with my ideas, I seek to leave behind the seed of my willingness in our union. Taking you within this blessed embrace, I penetrate your vulnerability. In the womb opened by our coupling, roots extend, creating fissures in the vessel adorned with innocence. The gown you wore the night before cannot shield the falseness you covet. The lace labors to hold together tenuous chastity. It becomes taught, then weakens, by the process of coming under the auspices of covenant. This sexual touch flashes, it blinds you to the person you thought you were. Ashamed by the swiftness white sheets turn red, you fight to put the dress back on, and all the while I guide you with my resolve. My words don't reach ears unwilling to come to term with the way my touch moves beyond sight, and the garden in your belly is made fertile in the light of darkness. This wedding, the portrait being torn like a cloud striking out violently over the sea, no one bears witness. It is happening, the poison seeping with intent, makes skin oiled and softened in youth decay. Tomorrow, you will reach for a mirror to confirm your fears. "I have become hideous with shame. His words, his manhood, has wrought a barrow of my virginity where nothing beautiful will I see. Must I look? Lifting the polished plastic is like you are being entombed. Inch after inch the angle catches your image. Earth chokes you with assumption. Anticipation makes you shake, and the dirt solidifies the grave. A headstone is placed over the eyes. Its shadow is like the writing carved in effigy. It reads, 'Once fucked. She died, living again, married to the fucker.' Eyes open, hearing the voice of your husband. The mirror reflects something unexpected. Instead of being ugly, you are something new and it is beauty. That grave was really a chrysalis. Metamorphosis takes place under the archway of our vows. However intolerable, they emerged in light of day. We find them good. When ready, the infant in your womb will enter a family where it is prepared by shearing off a carapace made hard by fear; It shines and thought perfect, but it is burning upon the altar. The ritual is time. It is full of fucking. You thought wrong, and after marrying progress you perceive its grace. Accepting the terms, it is part of your soul, for it was always your destiny to give birth to something new. Purified by rigors of internal struggle, this newness is sublime as a star discovered where you never thought to look.

Woman

Iconic stands the walls she builds. Raising as she goes
to market; like livestock parading atop her sisters' breast.
Streetlights were minor luminaries monitoring her
with their CCTV pornographic lenses—piercing veils, leering
with un-consensual motives. Shaping our daughters,
glances are unsaid catcalls. Meaning to lure,
as much as check the teeth of his chosen mount,
they are indiscriminately penetrating her. A power-struggle
where his fingers are tight. Around her neck, dignity torn,
the idol Beatrice ascends from her bondage in purgatory.
That place is for girls. Women sew embroidered sashes
with more scars than badges. This fabric is hidden, like her innocence,
but likewise, she must be mended after rending. With shakily, clenched fists
women rise to meet a world lying and bent. Eyes to the ground,
so maybe they pass right by, and notice nothing—
Like a prayer,
while she wears hajibs of downcast looks and baggy clothes,
so, they become ignorant to her. She doesn't exist at the grocery store
and the size of her waist is not an invitation.

The snakes in her hair burrow into her mind, this is self-defense;
doubts only overcoming fear by flipping through pages,
glossy magazine leaves where girls cut themselves,
because emotional stability isn't talked about
in locker room lullabies. Knives telling a lengthy narrative,
coercing the youth to believe
blood is the stain of maturity,
like it was a rite of passage.
Those girls, too brave for courage,
they seemingly swallowed pills
for taming the womb. It is an everyday pharmaceutical assault
where women drink the blades potion. Lips curling above the edges,

a nervous smile doesn't mean weakness. That would be tears,

that, and passersby don't collect them in their jars

the way girls bathe in them. Forever inside those Grey-water bathhouses

for girls only clubs. They teach His myth,

that gash between the legs means fragile.

"You are meant to be broken"—The mothers say,

and to their sons in hushed tones,

"As others, while blaspheming in the Goddesses' temples,

leave space for habitual desecration."

Children of a Dead-Waltz

In the wake of my footsteps, stamping their smoky rhythm

on the dancefloor. It is where vessels contort like pots boiling over

the square, light-up mosaic. Caving into primordial movements, as layers shed to

temporary housing on the chairs surrounding the ritual. Onlookers partaking

with a churning desire. The one lost to the playground

when your head can not squeeze through the gates. It is locked inside

that wall. I never climb anymore

because there is a desperation to that image.

The snapping sound from the kitchen was a novelty of anger

expressed in the broken cutting board in my father's hands;

The pieces of my brother, lying there on the linoleum,

like the puzzle of what would become of them. There was his missing piece

under the hand his body curled up around—it was ephemeral.

Something severed there along the veins. I had felt it,

watching them struggle to breathe,

through the fear.

He learned to walk soft,

we all did.

We left something in that house besides the reptiles buried in the backyard.

We danced, a black waltz.

In the background, I looked to my brother until he left,

then I came to know friends that were my own, not inherited

from traditional footpaths. We diverged,

but untimely, the echo escaped my throat

when we said goodbye…

I still left the back door open, half ajar. Silhouetting of the moon with that pane,

crossing into the night light. A cold wind crept in

the things we dreamed about in adolescence,

like a magazine pitch—leading to hotel stays

where the chauffeur drops you off in the hills.

So, he waited outside opportunity listening for the jingle of the doorknob.

But those words she destroyed him with slammed into focus

each time the door paralleled the sound. He played a new tune:

"Searching for the right one"; "the right block"; "a new home."

His voice cracked like porcelain on record

because those imaginary polaroid's

existing within the reverb in the vocals, if nowhere else.

His music has always moved me beyond wherever I am

to his side. I would linger again if I could. My arms are stretched

always around my brother…

My heart is heavy, but he outran our burden

"Capturing it again.

Locking it away in the lyrics,

a tomb with gilded edges."

There are bloody rivulets on the record. Every time

I am brought to acknowledge

they don't follow the grain of our scars.

That crimson sound is gone

when I see him on-stage. Something else calls out

to me. It welcomes me home.

Waking Embers

Sleeping through the alarms, we become shades of light dispersed by the drapes,
lingering and encased; asleep to the apparent
when my lids open. The mound beside me takes shape.
The scent of sweat and breath, like twelve years making love in that room—
This woman awoke my curiosity,
my conscience and passion. She wrapped it up in a smile
the way moments are caught up in the belly,
tearing away through the insides. She hid away my discontent
when I knew,
I wanted her to sleep next to me, forever.
That attraction raw and a curse; a feverish kind of love
whence I could never untangle myself. She unmade me
with her voice. She showed me,
she knew in a few words, I was more than my façade
styled in the manner of thieves. But I did steal her to my side
by vow. Our doubts disappearing like paper on the campfire,
our shapes blossomed into being embraced by one flame.

I remember when the snows could not stop her coming
on weekends. From Phoenix,
in a beat-up Taurus, to stay on my couch. I needed her;
she moved me in ways I can't forget.
Those curves were drawing others close, but I snatched her
like a cutpurse cutting the pockets of their victims,
pulling her into a hand she never noticed.
All the while her breath caught frost as it left her lips,
her voice a constant reminder that I would press them close
in my dreams. I was with her
in a garden of Pine. My ardor grew to new heights.
The weight of my branches heavy in my white scrawny limbs;
the load I carried would break any lesser woman.
There was so much strength in those pools of emerald eyes,

styling her face as something divine. The square tiled frieze arranged to match
her outline. It was what drew me into her shadow. There I was consumed
by her melody. I knew the chords she spoke in
when speaking to friends and singing with me. In subtle ways
the vibration grew intense over time. The pitch wavering
with the years passing. There became three (4) of us,
and while I would have to divide my heart,
the pieces coming apart like a Russian doll,
I never could tell which took the bigger piece.

I found I had more
blood pumping longer—harder—beating down my door,
unafraid, she stepped into view
through the cracks in my mind. When fear overtook me,
I remember the message on my phone; every time I turned it on,
"Stay together."
A period placed over the hole inside, scribbled there
in her hand. She filled her words with light,
leading me back.
Those visits, our hands together as anchors hanging on
below the rising waters, they tied knots around us
though I fought their hold. Again,
I lost my stubbornness in her words
pushing my fever to break. Her hands scrambling over the ropes,
pulling me to daylight. It was dreamlike—soft, as my skin
when I walked out of the hospital. The darkness left behind
when they could no longer feel my weight. Inside those doors
we left flakes of my insecurity floating between the sliding glass,
"surface."

Finding its way into the crawl space,
the scenes never fade where I store them;
on my wrist, pulling my chin down to look at a picture,
shaming me into focus, they are papercut reminders

scaring young skin, as festerous lesions are apt. Taking their time

healing, as trees do. I lost a couple of branches

touching others, close to their bole. Each time

more dropped away, and I found there were two constants:

    The light my companion grew my height by,

            its luster is always radiant.

    And the dark soil, deep around my roots,

It chokes me with the grasp of memories

hands, as concrete as the stakes pinning my wings.

Only moths, the shape of my bark, fly around her,

as I spread my limbs waiting for her fire to ignite their wool.

Because trees pray for lightning strikes,

they are united by it with the sky.

Leaves pray for the burning flame.

Their bursting color would rather ride the wind for a heartbeat than wither

upon the forest floor. I pray,

that light reaches me everyday

when I pull back the drapes and look at her shape.

Intermission

Between the cassette rollers recording, my brother's hand quivered
over the button. There is providence when the track starts. Fingertip in length,
it mirrored something in the music; that, we both aspired to capture.
That radio show started something in us on replay every Saturday night.
It was a time we had to agree which songs to keep—backpedaling the tape
otherwise. We would scramble over rewind and play,

        trying to cue it before
the next song started. I was alone in the record store, watching the register,
using the player, I bought 100min tapes—passing time on the needle up front,
while my lighter was used for Don's needle in back.
Bauhaus videos played on an ancient TV. Above the register,
there, hung Beatles bootlegs in wax; cornered in paper
with a pin piercing the plastic sleeve. It served as an escape,
a home away from the world; Made of wax, plastic, and music.

What is Upstairs?

I look at the entrance to my attic. In there, I can perceive this place
and other's. Houses like these, hidden and remote from daylight,
they are kept to the corners; Sharp when you peel back the plastic coating,
heat floods the rafters all year round. Making opaque my reasons,
my stream of doubts start to flood the living room. It becomes dangerous
close to the roof, too near the angle waxen wings melt. I guard my steps beam by beam,
but the dance to avoid pitfalls makes me dizzy. A calypso melody, forward and behind
my intent is rarely clear because I have trouble speaking
whilst I should be silent—
listening…
But I read it, disassembling my internal matrix, like a zombie automaton.
I sit at your table, but I am somewhere else. Working in the attic
an author\publisher\editor of self. Giving into my narrative—
Afraid to take too much for granted. The web above my head stretches
into the dark, and beyond the scope of my vision. A moment,
then depth snaps into meaning, as sweet and smokey as the mountain afire.

Mirrors and Silence

I see the mirror, and I hear those razor-sharp edges
flickering away at the border. Now it comes full circle
and the man I see I have little love for. He is weak
in person, strong on paper, but I want to throw his baggage
in the street.
That bend beyond my focused reflection's surface,
I want to reconcile what is missing.
This is a garment placed between me and the foreground.
A step through the windowsill, is my quiet refrain--
It has become my invulnerability, where I watch
the wheels still
the engine on the track, hissing against my restraint.
The train has grown restless, but I placed my thumb against it,
thoughts drawn against steel--crumbling like paper mache,
because something was refined in time. To assuage my guilt,
that train does not stray far. Its line's rehearsed
in another voice.

"It is a deafening song, wherein I fought
the machines of guilt," I said tasting the Sun.
I was humbled by my own imperfection
and my reach became a rendezvous with oblivion.

Throwing Rocks at Goldfield Ghost-Town

The saloon style doors of that bar didn't fit. The measurement was off.
Aye, the customer base was swollen. The rains brought it on—
the drunkard Ship-Captains who sailed there
between the vales of scarcity, I have heard their gravelly voices tell,
"O' treasures cast into the dunes; When the Sun, high, casting no shadows,
whispered where no winds blew." To them.
It was the light, that incessant friend
that guided both their course, and their thirsts.
For time is spelled out in its beatific path, carving fate in that wake.

"You will only descend into the canyon once more," I tell them,
bringing their supply for the winter tide—
A haboob whose dust would sap that strength early,
    but who listens to the bartender,
        one who only remembers the toads coming alive 12 Summers
           and they don't sing no more.
    Only the dry, caked earth on your boots tells you this salt isn't the same.
A lone Cactus Wren wings West chasing daylight,
like the fish have gone to warmer waters; The bats flock around stadium lighting
feeling that artificial breeze sucking the plankton almost into their waiting maw.

"How many has that canyon swallowed?" I almost don't.
I do not want to look at who I am asking. Looking up from cleaning
the dust off full glasses, I see
the place is empty. Only the hulls of their ships, bellies full of strong liquor
remaining. It is the shadow of the Desert Kingdom.
And I just pour the drinks.

Rattlesnake

I shy away from drunkenness, having tasted being forgetful on the back of my throat. I can see behind me the light catches the mirror. It stirs the hair on my neck, casting a shadow before me I do not always recognize. Holding onto my reflection—I see my crows feet take flight from my eyes and enter the invisible bandwidth of history. It is bright back there. I want to draw the shades, but they cut my fingers in alarm. "Less we forget," they hiss sliding back and forth in sibilant confusion. The snakish sound twists and grows. I hear a poisonous rattle on the tail-end of the liturgy, warning me to watch my step every time I think about the past.

A Holy Place

I took your picture, across from that hallowed street.
The one birds continually sang in the tree.
The sand is cool against our bare feet, while fruit we smelled
somewhere in the deep recesses of true desire;

I processed the chemical reaction.
Pardes was spiritous, surrounding us.
Lifting our faces to acknowledge grace amongst the flowers—
Miraculous I tasted its nectar amongst the thorns;

I am old, laying a photograph beside my love.
My memories of her are still bold, as she leaves in peace.
But Her Memoir is scrawled dark on paper as soft as buttermilk,
in a place in my heart, I dare not silence.

Floating Through the Monsoon

I once had a dream about floating
palm fronds piled up amongst the sands of the canal,
currents flowing deadly below, I walked out onto that aluminum
railway, ten feet above the water. It was right down my street,
where metal shudders as it slinks across
this river. It is the life of the desert city
and it will claim our bodies in the end,
like clouds to coax our faces towards Heaven.

When that young man skated by with a plastic, garbage bag.
the leaves of foreign trees were caught up by an exodus,
flying down the storm's gale. Picking up speed,
that boy caught in his arms the Western Wind Demon.
The Sun barely a witness to its capture
through the diffuse light and ahead of the storm.
Floating...
above, the horizon as rain began gathering around the edges;
Streetside gutters irrigated the driveway entrances, making ponds
instead of intersections, where all those land-locked automobiles were
creeping across the skirt, watery legs spinning without traction.
He rode towards the sunset, stopping for convenience
at the store on the corner.
Next to the adult cabaret for preschoolers to lie about,
drinking a beer where those strippers tossed cigarette butts.
the men at the door gave his net stony glares, but he hadn't crossed the line
where women in lingerie and less were slicking back their hair.
Goosepimples rose up their legs to flower around thighs,
holding wallets in lace. They were bulging, thick, but he left his eyes off,
on the sky's curtains in the east. It always rained more on that side,

somehow; it is a war across Central,

where the train saws across the valley's belly. It sounds a horn triumphant,

as thunder follows the electric current, turning west.

Past the Papago, it's fury rides ahead carrying the invaders war cry,

scoring the mounds with a lost melody.

With a bow raised by the thumbs, that kid slides across Campbell,

flowing towards sunset, pulled by black sails.

Dream Stranded

On my way to work, I rode my bicycle across the bridge into the city. Right away people were slowing me down; the pedestrians clogged their crossing, surrounding two large news vans and the blue and red flashing lights. I got off my bike and approached the yellow, "NO CROSSING," tape. A police officer saw me approaching and lifted the divider, ushering me inside the crime scene. Why didn't I stop?

Not minding my business, I asked him, "Wouldn't I get in the way?" His eyes crossed over me. I asked him, "What happened?" His flashlight comes off his belt, and assuming violence, I lurched onto the scene. "Why would I…"

A step inside, the Sun is on the other side of the bridge. I even remember remarking on it, but this is today and that is the Sun in the East. I turned, "Where did those cops go? The ambulances? Where are the people?" My voice carried and because this place could really make you think, you are alone, like there was no other sound in the world to muddle the message. You might call out? I did not.

I saw him, me. There I was, elbows on the railing. Looking at me, I felt cold; that part of me looking so warm. There were puddles forming in the shadows of that architecture. I was in the mirror universe surrounding my feet. That version: Me--He must be a jumper. I thought about that, but I remembered that ghosts do not think. Maybe mirror recognition jolts the periphery.

The Sun at that moment was on replay, ever giving. I thought about crying and I was gasping for air, my tears drowning me. I could not move. I was the darkness floating around my bodily debris, washing out to the ocean.

On my way to work I rode my bicycle across the bridge, into the city. Right away people were slowing me down; the pedestrians clogged their crossing, surrounding two large news vans and the blue and red flashing lights. I got off my bike and approached the yellow, "NO CROSSING," tape. A police officer saw me approaching and lifted the divider, ushering me inside the crime scene. Why didn't I stop?

[Unfinished] Breakfast

There are courses to life. Dining alone,
they taste different; it is as though you do not need to rush
through the syrup and pancakes, as I did as a child – then again.
There are things about breakfast I do not find at the diner,
with servers pouring at least 3 cups of coffee. The Eggs tasting stale,
as the smoke of my cigarette makes its way into the non-smoking section,
the ash at the tip lingering, clinging to the ember stoking its affectation.
  There is a ringing attached to the sway of the glass door slamming.
That weight crashed into the crumbling door jamb; the sheet rock was pressed,
discolored, and worn down to primer grey. My smoke lingered in the air,
and within bubbles of the chocolate milk. My straws trapped and released spirits
whom evaporated upon my whims' leisure. Like a strike of violence,
the first course is hurt…

To be Brief

The hot cocoa reminded me, I spilt boiling water onto my brother's chest,

when we were young. He blew out his lungs and almost suffocated in front of me.

I told them to call an ambulance, while he writhed on the floor

nails raking his throat.

No one moved—silence, except for me

breathing into my brother because he could not.

He got up, and we went back to school.

Like that is normal—Like anything ever is

Heard in Temple Walls

They called me urchin—I remain a mouse
touring the fields; not speaking aloud
I find medicine in words, where they appear in mind.
A vision unadorned, only the things my writing defines.
I was once lost in a sheet, unable to breathe
with the minute lungs of rodent size. I was elsewhere deceased,
when I looked upon that sheet. it made senses fire;
everything inside became water, conforming to desire.
That is where life can falter—
When ego is sired, it accuses the Deceiver,
Believer and Cleaver. They have crossed the steeper steps
to conquer emotions and ask for requests,
but a mouse is not invited inside. I go below—
my place sidled beneath the foundation long ago.
How may I serve a master so big? His first step is over my head
And my reach is so small, the grass dwarf's me;
even it is not very tall. Compared to the steps of the Seas
it cannot holdfast, it would be obliterated,
like the prairie was inundated.
Nothing is impossible for He shaped Man
out of the ground. He made them many nation
carved in blood. Saturated,
this field's bosom takes in their kindred,
like a widow, a shepherd, a forlorn soul—
They were taller than the step, but they are buried below.

They call me wretch—I live under-foot
where casually I stretch, below, where no toe above wears soot.
There songs reverberate those boards overhead,
like my whole world shook, causing catastrophe; raising the dead.

There is something in their voice, a timbre of a sort.

It locks onto me, lifting me into states of ecstasy.

I let escape a squeak along with it. Reflecting on its melody

the two became one transfixed, but those inside seem to feel,

by the lip tight hum and peel,

something for them making their G-d so real.

I must be lacking.

It could be something integral to life that a mouse does not partake in.

I hear them facing me, whispering to the underground, nearest to their bent knee;

every parting of their lips is like the Sun pouring down— trusting in me,

our lives become intimate, but my own voice is meek

as I try to tell G-d, "I am more than cheap fleece.

Like any man, I need to believe, I am greater than my parts in total."

But without that kind of spirit a mouse is not immortal.

Beneath: The Dark Sun

We were playing in the heat. The sweat between our toes,
it made us want to take our shoes off,
but the thought of wet socks on tile brought us back.
To the game, our thumbs drifted across the pads
scraping the pattern of the future; one that was always
changing in the generations, like that number of revolutions
spelled something magical about what you were to do, then.
He changed at 8. And we didn't see it right away.
My pattern lost apparently when I saw him look away,
it became obvious something was distant.
I asked him and he didn't answer me, like my words were water
slipping out my mouth and down my shirt—never making it to him.
That is the feeling enabled inside. The barrier between us,
he slips behind it, but there are holes there.
I feel the pressure building and without a fracture…

The AC is on the fritz, and our shirts come off.
We take turns dunking our heads in the shower,
to cool off. Sugar water comes out of the freezer
reclaiming our boredom in front of the T.V.
I ask him, "where do you go? When the lights go off?"
All I get is looks.
He tells me, "It's all feeling. Like sinking."
Like the game I guess, for him its intuition,
even though we do not see the layer come off. We know
the feeling changed. It has gotten cooler.
He's not in the dark, if he can still feel the Sun.
        I can reach him in his silent fortress.
We turn off the Game. Taking a hurried drive to Grandma's,
we scurry in her wooden, slat gate.
The 10min drive was sweltering and changing into suits,
it is instantaneous.

I clean the bugs out with the net,

feeling the splash of lukewarm water against my ankles.

He can't wait to get in, but there is a danger there wasn't before.

We play in the shallow end in the late afternoon,

as the matriarch cooked and talked with mom on the porch.

We can smell the stench of mediocre pozole as he slips

into the background, underneath. Where I quickly pull him to the side.

I am afraid as he comes too, coughing.

With each breath I am going inside, checking on him

with something akin to controlled panic.

I lingered near him with eager resolve,

but some layers we cannot shed.

Some revolutions bring the unexpected,

the heat of those days is a dreadful, piercing magic.

The Icy Photograph in the Airport Lobby

There is frost on the wind. When you breathe my name
the cold sound strikes, like a crackle
around an icicle surrendering its long hold. I can smell the spring
in your step—smashing the pond where I learned to skate
trying to trap me under the ice; sunlight is never kept from the clever cages.
Those windows have locks that look like Nobel Prizes, and the grades you got
in school. We were forced to announce our allegiance
without the thought ever crossing our minds.
To bear arms for those purple mountains, grand.
        To shed blood of Man for fabric's ties of brotherhood
which means a great deal to great men, but their sons do not join the ranks.
Breathe my name again, too;
hold up my brother and not bury his shell. For those caskets don't keep out the snow
melting into the ground. Let old hatreds disappear
as your propelled into a new season. Let nature lay flowers
upon the desert path. Pile rocks to show the two sides of time,
that mountain pass is not the distant horizon. Thing is, we keep that place in a frame
on the wall, where we land in airplanes. We're trapped beneath that icy glass.
I'm in the lobby getting Starbucks, and my ticket says, 'Anywhere,'
else.
Breathe my name in the heat of summer. With sweat on your lips
and thirst sated not far from your grasp, cause convenience began
when the train stopped here in the valley. It used to be Mexico,
we walked nations of people we used to kill, here; told them to stay,
like dogs under the knife—Their future bleak and not chosen.
Tell me the desert is your home and I'll ask if you have seen the coyote,
fighting the monsoon with tooth, heat, and pressure.
That war that he fights is because he only sees the ground where he buries his prey
And he never looks at the stars.
Breathe my name like a wolf at the Moon if the hunt continues
tomorrow night. For that sky is not far from the vision we share
beneath the fur and within the blood

our clot packs the wounds of fragility in the world.
Streetlights can only illumine the bones beneath
the lamps glow—Winter is a season of luminescence
but it hides something under that luster, as does the process of time.
It is not always creating diamonds without conflict. But it doesn't take catastrophe
to taste the wind and know the chatter spells genocide,
or to look at the market and know people will die without food
cause America sets the price of the world.

"Don't breathe," they said.
"The longevity of breath is minimal, so do not abide in it.
Gold holds value longer than breathing lungs.
Don't talk either!"

The Latticework Outside the Window

When you are fixing your make-up tomorrow, I will linger
in your shadow. I am there in the reflection; it is a candid moment,
us caught between the reality and the mirror. You are drawing on your eyeliner,
it is the most I look into your eyes, and I am sorry for that.
You got it right. I didn't always pray at this goddess' temple
in earnest. Longevity holding us together like concrete, but I am afraid too,
staring too long at the church you paint with a steady hand.
It isn't that those stars, woven there, do not keep me up all night. They do.
The attraction has not subsided—over the years
we came together in our most trying moments,
and I do not know how else it could have worked out.
Through the forest or open plain, avoiding the potholes is easy,
so instead, it was the winding mountain pass that we chose,
where one summit begat more in the distance,
separated by deep valleys. The unspoken reality
as we march through obstacles, our hands were coming together
in new ways. It wasn't what I had expected from ardor,
since I had tasted loves venom.
The recourse when I could feel its pull, wearing a different body,
you have become the Sun on my face.

Singing in the car until the mood can't take anymore away from us,
like those harmonies, it appears we are out of tune;
the feeling I get is what a fly experiences in the fan just outside
the grocery store, when the allure of your appetites flavor desire
to go inside. The mirth of your smile speaks
to me—between the mystery of your lips
you are screaming. The words attached to a yearning
to break through my walls. You have built ladders to the top
when the siege became the attrition of 12 years,
you realized throughout the destruction, you had misunderstood
I am the cover on the book.

And it is not really the series you set out to read,

but you read it all in my vows. And I meant them

when I said forever. I saw the words, I hoped had taken root

in your heavens. The echo in our hearts,

it is not something distant.

It rings out, though my body

to the very stem of my passion

when I find my voice, placing it here between the spelling.

Like the borders around your eyes,

I hope I fill them up until you fall in love with my characters.

I feel you there, in ways that cannot find expression,

but I try. The ears I have are not always

catching you breathing sparks to kindle my fire,

but I wished to, in the days past.

Then, I was too stubborn to show

I love you so much

even though I have been behind you

this whole time. I have wanted to be center stage,

having written our story thus far. The future seems amazing

when it is there. In front of Us,

that ocean I can't cross without you.

    Once, the hard ground was a home. Our summer there

in the woods. We would work in town

passing elk migrating across traffic. On that drive

we sped past the lakes erupting fog, those white beards

telling of wisdoms heat there beneath the covers,

showing us the signs to slow down. Time stopped at Ashurst,

overgrown with pine. To take the needles of life away

from where you laid our tent, I saw

a different sort of attraction. We made love in the moonlight

on the back of your car. The stars rolled through the Ether

to the choir singing on the radio. If anything,

the light illumined your skin

with my touch. You brought the heat to my tent

and although it was short-lived, the forest came alive

in those months.

The next season we were back south. The desert

drinking our youth with a thirst that is not satisfied.

I tried to leave then. We sat on the back porch

holding each other. Tipping over in a corduroy recliner

I smiled at you, but my eyes betrayed my misgivings.

It was wrong, that smile, the thoughts inside

playing the scenario— "without you."

On my ship when it carried me away:

> To graze on pastures green in the summer

> To watch the ground, soaking up the souls of wheat…

> …listening to the rictus sheading of seed;

for all of you called out, but I could feel ashes upon the wind

as Winter draws frost, biting my ears;

it was burning desire blurred between us.

I am the darkness slipping across the paper map back to you,

but the wake of my reach creased my course. Dividing us,

I tried to correct my image,

but you never spoke to the mirror I bent satisfying vanity.

Your attention was on Me, cutting through all the layers

no matter how intricate. I made the shadows around the features.

You emboldened me to reach for the light

I could not reconcile. The bleeding in my chest

when you told me you loved me too,

that word hurts the most

whenever I used it. I meant it.

Winter's sting abating, like that stare could cut right through me,

into the stormy waters I am constantly returning to drown beneath.

It is the feeling that I would lose her,

that has become bitterly familiar. A sulfurous pocket

close to the ocean floor, because in that place,

that of regrets, and guilt—apathy grows.

I dropped anchor there, to stare at your city, too far from the shore.

So, I couldn't hear the warmth of your hearth singing, but through the cracks

below the waterline fissures, let my body's heat rise to the surface

every time I feel you pressed against me. I hope that is where you want to be.